A CIVIC PAGEANT

A CIVIC PAGEANT

A CIVIC PAGEANT

Frank Montesonti

Black Lawrence Press
New York

Black Lawrence Press
www.blacklawrence.com

Executive Editor and Art Director: Colleen Ryor
Managing Editor: Diane Goettel
Book Design: Steven Seighman

Black Lawrence Press
8405 Bay Parkway C8
Brooklyn, N.Y. 11214
U.S.A.

"Every 1930's French Novel" appeared in *Black Warrior Review*.
"Heaven's Undershirt", "Train Ride to Yourself in Handcuffs", and "One Last Waltz on an Ave Maria" appeared in *Spork*.
"Quitclaim of the Wizard of OZ" first appeared in *Poet Lore*.
"Piranha" appeared in *Nimrod*.
"Gratuitous Voice-Over at the End of a Film Reflecting on the Tribulations of the Plot and Coming Finally to an Epiphany" appeared in *Cream City Review*.
"The Incalculably Long Geometry of Sobriety" appeared in *Green Mountain Review*.
"Redundancy of Light" and "Dark Matter Theory" appeared in *Alaska Quarterly Review*.
"Faking It" appeared in *Barrow Street*
"A Flock of Iagos Waiting in the Wings" appeared in *42 Opus*.
"Film Noir" appeared in *Poems and Plays*.
"A Time to Sing of Airports" appeared in *Slipstream*.
"Those Anomalies at a Party When Everyone Falls Silent" appeared in *DIAGRAM*.

Published 2009 by Black Lawrence Press, an imprint of Dzanc Books

First edition 2009

Printed in the United States

Contents

Gratuitous Voice-Over at the End of a Film, Reflecting on the Tribulations of the Plot and Coming Finally to an Epiphany

Then I realized, rowing across the lake,
    that even if mother never leaves the sanitarium
and they build another aviary and free the bullfinches
as drops of yellow paint into the sky,
the sun survives, and if I get another postcard
from some port from a sailor who might be
my father, and if Jessica decides to forgive me for my comment
in the lighthouse as our silhouettes were broadcast
like two conjoined giants on the midnight-purple sea,
and if we recover the petrified cat
from the soup and ash of the house,
if all this were to happen,
rowing across this lake with the trees in their
last struggle of color as the cold opens a hole in the sky
and the water hardens to glass –
I thought about Charles at the Café de Flore
smoking Gauloises and watching the ankles of girls
young as blue flowers, the world never runs out,
though we choose someone to love above the rest
and get down to defining or dying –
Claire and the shining
woman alighting from the jewelry store,
winter rain cutting through tree branches,
all this inevitable turning in my life,
a tornado kicking out shreds of barn,
or an icebreaker ship rolling like an oily bell.
It's as if there's a camera that pans out farther
and farther until you question what holds it.
Then I realized, rowing across the lake,
that there's so little to keep me from sinking,
just this small craft,
suspended above the consuming water.

The Incalculably Long Geometry of Sobriety

November always starts out this way:

you feel like a box, then you feel trapped in a box.

A week since my last drink. The falling from the high blue I
was, was more crystalline in the memory than climbing spiral
apartment staircases in Chicago.
                    It's called a *flight of stairs*
because you're rising. You feel like a movie,
rapping on someone's door,

then you're in a movie.
You could swing the camera around and watch the brickwork
of snow.

I'm going to miss the winter,
how it throws a white sheet over the lawns and caps
the trashcans. How it expects

us to wait like starved doves under a magician's cape
for the disappearing. It will hurt the first time you look

at the winter and the *winter in us.*

Out there, in the snow is a kid in a blue sweater with a head
full of bronze gears
who is trying to grasp the incalculably long geometry
of loss and life. I'll miss him too.

But not having the shakes so bad,
stumbling by bungalow-style houses spiked with ice,
it seemed the world would shatter.

Today, under the cold

and overcast sky I go to the laundry room to buy another soda.
O Loneliness.
I love the staged heartbeat of a Coke shouldered from the machine.

A Flock of Iagos Waiting in the Wings

On a bridge in Indianapolis
   I'm getting covered with coils of snow
like George Bailey (Jimmy Stewart) in *It's
a Wonderful Life* before he wishes he

was never born and then is swallowed
whole by an alternate universe
like a snake unhinges its jaw and admits
even the bones. So, sans George, the ursine

winter took his brother's life, the druggist
went to prison for dispensing rat poison
instead of aspirin and no kindly bank
offered affordable mortgages, so the town

was constricted (financially) then choked
out by cheap neon from the luminous
vices. Every time I watch the film my heart
feels like Lucifer in a tree when I realize

how, just because George reneges on his wish,
this whole other earth will be erased,
the decent man turned snake oil salesman
will lose the brief venom of visual exultation

of a *Live Girls* sign high on gin
when George is born again. I read this article
about some scientists who theorized
twenty ways the world might end

and the last way was: Someone wakes up
and finds it has all been a dream. Yes, this trick
is cheap soap opera tripe, but who says
we live in an expensive universe? On NOVA

I saw the story of a man with a condition
called the Capgras Delsion who believed

all his loved-ones were carbon-copy imposters.
He wasn't frightened; he didn't think his parents

were reptiles in rubber suits or Iagos waiting
in the wings, rubbing their elderly hands;
they just weren't *them*. He even referred
to himself as the *other* David. I'm standing

on a bridge in Indianapolis watching the legless
moonlight, the legless snow, snake
through the wind, worried, the marriage might
carry off the ether that holds us down.

In the winter, this is a humorless city,
and behind me cars strike through the slush.
I'm not thinking of doing anything drastic;
I'm just watching the light from the nearby power

plant occasionally coil in a divot of water,
shine like a scale, and then disappear.

Every 1930's French Novel

Someone will be named Boris and although
he is a friend he must come to be despised.
Mathieu will wash his feet before making love.
There will be much ado about Proust and crab lice.
Peter will see his woman, the long malaise
of her stomach wide as Boris' sardonic grin;

suddenly he *loathes* her, the scene turns grim,
she pleads, begs, kisses his feet, although
she knows they will make love, their limbs a malaise
like tears on a street corner. Despite
all he says, he adores her back, the licentious
way it dips softly and rises like love.

Daniel or Mathieu will find he doesn't love
himself enough to kill himself, or face the grim
morning. Someone will have to be deloused.
Boris puts two fingers of water in Pernod although
it makes Ivich wince and makes Andree despise
him. The Seine is a crepuscular malaise

at twilight. Through the unending malaise
of Free Will someone will choose to love
the person, who at the start, they most despised.
A prostitute will have a scar the shape of a grin.
The most idiosyncratic wins, although
he will probably acquire crab lice

in the process. Yet to have crab lice
is a wonderful red badge in the malaise.
Poor Sartre didn't even believe in Free Will although
he was admired for trying to love
the great, greasy edges of the Lords grin.
Many, many will be disillusioned but despised

is another matter, nobody ever despises
another for more than a candle's second. The lights

blink on and off in their grimaces
and smiles. A hunchback, the Malaysian
drifter who makes Marie cry, they love
to show up in the plaza although

they will eventually disappear, lice ridden and despised.
Although they will represent the lost love,
the solitary grin, the last bolt of light in the malaise.

Redundancy of Light

Outside this hotel room
rain falls as pure as its definition.
Call the French, tell them

there should be a word
for shadows of raindrops
on a hotel window.

Scientists say that if you could hear your own
heartbeat you'd slowly go insane.
I lay on the floor and the shadow rain

moves over my skin as I listen
to something bigger than my one heart:

billions of people
and their loneliness
rising like humidity.

I wish they would put a shot of whiskey
next to the Bible
in every hotel drawer
so I could warm to the idea
of living forever.

More shadows, more rain,
a pump, bigger and as constant
that I can't turn off.

Trees step out of their shadows.
A few cars make incisions in the skin of water
on the road, but they heal.
They always heal. If, I mean when,
you also realize yours
is the only heartbeat you cannot hear,
I need to tell you something before it's too late:
It's too late.

Dark Matter Theory

They say that only 1% of the galaxy is
made of stars 5% heavy gasses
and planets. Less is garbage dumps
on Rhode Island, gulls crying in compassed

circles, and very little statistically
your stockpile of French-cut
green beans gathering dust
slow as the Artic collects snow.

The rest of the *weight of the world*
is unattached subatomic particles, so small they can't
even reflect light. They flow between

the space between us – an ocean
we hardly notice because we are invisible
to most of what is out there. Sometimes a dark matter

particle collides with a visible particle
and the visible particle shakes. Imagine a man losing
his balance and careening

into a small tree. Imagine between each
tree a thousand miles.

In England a team of scientists are
deep in a mine, waiting for one
of these particles to shake an atom of rock.
Standing there, waiting for proof
that we can't even touch

two thirds of the universe;
They're just watching these otherwise-useless, nearly
priceless instruments: *O my soul!*

Blackout

The next morning,
 garlic bread, a glass of milk,
and a bowl of tuna salad,
lie untouched on the kitchen table.
I try to piece together
last night like a shattered black
vase: slow, and with attention to the eventual
healing. But all I suspect is that
there must be someone in me

more attractive than the self
I know: who *likes to cook, enjoys taste,*
who does not remember
the bad times, who, if you didn't want him,
would wake up the next morning,
someone else.

Those Anomalies at a Party when Everyone Suddenly Falls Silent

I love the illustrated medical books
where you can remove the transparencies:
epidermis, muscles, vital organs,
endocrine system, the upside-down
movie-screen that hangs on two ropes

in the back of the eye, the skeleton,
until there is just a crude black outline,
empty as a child's résumé. I was pleading
under the eve of the chemistry building,

when someone sapped the lightning
bivouacked in the clouds, burnt
the construction paper moon, font size
of the rain lessening, until I could barely say,

please don't leave, don't leave, don't.
Sometimes the silence lasts too long
and something lifts away all the layers until
I'm as empty as that field

by the high school, used for nothing,
but mowed so religiously in the summer.
Then the noise comes back; I watch a plane draw
a chalk line in the sky for God to cross

if he were really here, but the God of jealousy
and wrath must have floated off
in some globular lightning storm to another
universe. In middle-school the science

teacher would put up the transparency
of the orbits of the planets,
a big black finger coming in to flip away the earth.

Piranha

try to tell my students to use images:
say, a piranha eating an apple
or a piranha flying through the air
and biting a woman's jugular.

Maybe you could say that when the blood
sprays from the woman's neck it looks like, hmm,
a red Chinese fan.

When I'm asked what a poem should be like,
I simply state the fact that a full-sized cow can walk into a river
and a school of piranha can devour it in two minutes.

They work their way in the belly and eat out the soft organs.
Then the skin and head dance on top of the water.

Frank, do all our poems have to be about piranhas?
a student asks – the piranha.
No, no, not if you don't want them to be about piranhas,
I tell her, of course
I really don't see the point
of not writing about piranhas:

that moment when the water starts to break and pop
before the frenzy.

Heaven's Undershirt

Imagine a beach where the waves fold into curls of damaged brightness and white houses stretch down the hill to a kind of eternity. I'm there, a shape abstract enough to be all I remember in this life. Hail thwacks on umbrellas. Hail rebounding off the street making long skewed checkmarks.

Impressionistic swirls of daybreak through window screens. Noise pooled in the divots of sand. A blackbird on the cleaning table lifts the skin of a walleye.

My dreams begin in an overgrown field in Indiana. Fireflies spark in staccato flashes. Then the dark churns out FACES. In my dreams:

a diamond as big as a car.

Noise shot from a finite point. The sky steers the earth. A hand emerges from the noise then a silhouette then my jacket of cold. The waves broke into white static at the bar. Walking down the beach we looked like quarter notes from a distance.

Raindrops hit our skin, undid the old photographs in their bellies on the cool sand. A gull cried: *space smells like a fired gun.*

Something justifying about this beach, this lie, this hunger of gulls making strong brushstrokes above the sailboats' right triangles. The wind twined your hair into a lucent shape.

Our footsteps trailed behind us then pushed their signatures out.

My mother washing lake-water off her hands with tap water, cold and distant as herself. Each of the thousand lakes divines the vague blue of all things transitory, and she thinks she can work herself clean.

It's almost as if I'm in a place not quite a place, heaven almost. When you turn on a lamp stars are silent. Resting your head

on the cold car window. Christmas trees in living rooms.
Smell of gasoline in the marina.

Imagine Chicago. The same ejaculating fountain in the same
arc and the birds all hung with feathers and the sky all hung
with birds. Lives are silence. Only one light is on in death.

The crayon picture you drew of the two men carrying so many
rifles up the hill they could have been dying metaphorically.

The EL rattles pans from cheap studios. Go back to the
beach. No don't. Rivers keep flowing and some lesser-known
fraction comes to dominate the future.

Dear Reader. One night when I was still becoming a man,
the moon threw down its white wet underclothes on the tree
branches in my front yard

And since then I've been shocked.

So I tried to forget. To float away. A hiss of dark liquid and
I'd join the sky.
I don't love myself.

Two lawn chairs so close they're kissing. Traveling cross-
country I imagined the old Volvo that passed had a bumper
sticker that read, "Death Tastes Like Vanilla Wafers."

In the heart of man is how he disappears, holds himself to
fault and faults and loves the world too much. Locking up the
store, smoking, the dumpster smoking in the winter air, the
factories' big cigarettes.

A Cheetos bag flung against my leg outside the Arby's and I
sat down right there and thought about all the parking lots in
the world.

The lake has layers of cold. Hook a leech through its head.
My Bears jacket is flimsy. Half of the pockets of water are
filled with silver, others move in a darkness I must still be
coming to terms with.

The way an indoor pool opens like an orchid does with wavy
blue light on the ceiling.
If it's not too much to ask, I'd like to know something about you,
something dark. What motorcycle stunt would your heart be?

Easy. The woman in the sphere with the six cycles. Easy.
As you filed past me for the basketball game I could smell
vanilla following you.

In the library is a book called *The Third Treasury of the
Familiar* and nowhere in that book will you find a charcoal
sketch of your heart. Of the little, black, drunken skeleton
flung again and again against the wall of your ventricle.
Listen closer.

In the courtyard of my friend's apartment in Hollywood while
reading a book light fell on the page of verse and I read what was
underneath. Someone in their apartment was singing.

In an abandoned Sears parking lot I found a note, it read, *I
wish you were here but I'm glad you're not.* And I continued
watching the snow almost melt under the lot lights. I wrote
one back it read, *somewhere far away from you is another you.*

 So I mistook the child by weight for the phonebook. So I left
the cat on "Nap" all day.

The cup of coffee	(is)	a bomb
The falling snow	(in actuality)	someone drowning
Sorrow	(she forgot her)	red camel's hair
		coat on the chair.

If there are faces in the clouds they're cold and far away.

Tonight I stare into my blue eyes, at my ratty T-shirt, my uncut
haircut, into the moving of the water in that blue, that only
someone else will come to understand as the moving of my life.

Minnesota. Trees sound their alarms. I have dreams where
I'm in a moving relief, the foreground scenery pulled fast, the

trees a little slower, the sky barely moves at all and these are
the times I feel stuck in narration. The nearness of nearness.
Nightmares about riding on a shrinking train.

A dog vomiting up red letters by a dead bush. No one
understands a single night of their life enough to carve the
firework back from the explosion.

You wash your hands but you don't call it a kind of glove. I
mean, listen. A woman runs a squeegee down the coffee
shop window erasing the world from the window and all you
can do is go to the grocery store and puke your eyesight on
an orange.

A crane lifts a blue box into the blue sky. Rain makes holy
static on a lake. I had a long conversation with the green,
cubed, windshield glass on the street in the Bloomington
winter moonlight until you came and touched my shoulder.

Head trauma and the smell of caged crickets in a bait shop.
I'm beginning to take the correct number of drags from
my cigarette before I bend its body in half and snuff out its
hair. My dreams begin in an overgrown field in Indiana,
thousands of lightning bugs rising.

For in the abdomen of a lightning bug is an old man who
occasionally drops his lantern. Accident nears prayer. This
light rises

but does not leave the world, not quite. Night volleyball
games in summer. You and me in the corner of the party,
suddenly the distance between our lips, so many ellipsis dots
to subtract.

Wasp paranoia in campground restrooms. A wasp looks like
an old woman pulling a black jar across ice. In this stretch of
lies and birds overhead where dandelions spark in cold fields.
Pressing wet handfuls of sand through my fingers, storm
clouds pulling apart in their tongue and groove above Santa
Monica Pier. Your smudged silhouette in the wind almost

erased. Inside man is how he disappears, flashes on this
wide, wronged earth and lets his life go up and out.

The ocean looked like us all, heaved together in a dark beyond
thought. Look at me on bicycle, hair tossed in scriptures mad
and sick in brown moonlight. How do you die?

How do you write about failure at all?

Train Ride to Yourself in Handcuffs

1.

Nobody will untie you. As the train falls over each rail
and you're jarred to sleep. When you find that you're
the damsel tied to the tracks. As you walk down the long
lines of trees and lampposts

and wake on the same train. Hold on. Stop the poem.

We were both wearing white. The parade went by, pinwheels
on fire. It was easy
to lean into each other.

The noise from the parade rose forever.

2.

The idea scared the shit out of me. That quite possibly the world,
which I had heretofore considered only a large and lovely hat

might be real.

My white sheet looked clear. The Floridians brought juice
and pills to reduce the fever. Dreams stood up, lit cigarettes,
spoke a word or two of French and left
the drapes slowly clucking about the wind.

When I was sleeping the moonless blue

ocean broke off rocks. When I was sleeping
three gold rings were drawn around
the sun at daybreak.

Beads of sweat on my forehead with small anchors in them.

3.

James, me and the Greek girl with mayonnaised hair. Her
strangely tranquil lap dog. Pay campsites and a fiancé from
India? I couldn't imagine her life.

I nursed my 7:00 A.M. beer and we watched
the ferry dock. And the ocean looked like us all. Free,
except to exist. The ocean looked
like me. The ocean looked like a prison.

4.

Your eyes were blue like a Siberian Husky's – *Frank, that is
a Siberian Husky.* Oh, but it licked the back of my knee so
gently it could have been a rag of moonlight!

5.

If you're in Toledo clap your hands, in Houston, in San
Diego, and clap your heart
at night to stay alive. In history class so many years ago, at
the top of my skull was one
red biplane in an endless loft to my desire.

6.

Half my family is from the South. It's rumored we bleed in
the shape of Mississippi. The only shame whispered is of
great grandfather Trulove, who in the depression knelt in a
field and took his life with a shotgun.

I hear the echo rolling across the fields and down to the
river. A noise, a cloud of blood that must have held itself
intact before the wind marched the layers off.

Nobody etc...

Film Noir

Sunlight broke in the window.
I had the legal right to shoot it and ask questions later. She stood, hat eclipsing her face. "You've come highly recommended," she said, more insult than compliment.

This other life is comforting. But in the real world, a more universal plot brightens. I pull down one shade and focus on two pans balancing on the cold electric coils of my stove. I play a few chords on the piano to nobody.

It's only the film that makes the birds black and white, abstract, painted in simpler terms. Able to fly away and flying away.

You see, I'm after what's behind the low-budget scene where one shadow shoots another, behind what makes electricity jog around the socket after the power surge. I dream I have rectangles of skin stapled over my skin,

As if I'm trapped under some artifice and can't surface. I confirmed my suspicions: one day I found the rain was just someone spraying a hose against the window, the thunder just a big sheet of metal.

I'll be driving down 37 in Indiana and exit on 154th street in the Bronx, fifty years ago, holding up a picture at a gas station: "Have you seen this lady, a black Oldsmobile?" I polish my telephoto lens with a handkerchief as the cheating husband leans in the door of the hotel for a last kiss. I don't care if she looks as fresh as a cherry pie cooling on the windowsill for a starving god of cliché; she fits well on a negative that will develop into a positive on adultery.

Heaven's a difficult place to get into, but it's an open-book test. You can bring one note card written on front and back. God is kind. Explain the missile, heatstroke, Greek food. But walking from the car to the K-Mart, I feel like I'm in some lower house of heaven, as if a hand might pull out the keystone and everything, and the everything behind everything, will blink into rain.

Most of the work isn't exciting. My date tonight is the bottom forth of a fifth of rye whiskey. In the film, a woman in a long coat runs down to the bay, says, "The sky is an old book of names," seemingly to no one.

In the Blue Garter, the jewel-eyed singer visits each mobster's table, picks up their chins with her gloved hand but secretly glances at me, who knows form and fulfillment. Say it starts to rain. A silhouette darkens the soaped glass of my office and my cigarette brightens my face.

"It was raining. I had to come in," she says. And from that moment I know she's behind the brightness, so I unfold the light in the room and unfold my legs off the table, and lean forward into the unfolded light, and we unfold a few words, and she unfolds her hands.

You see, light goes out and out until my heart is lit up like a truck stop, until I feel like a detective who has forgotten why he was jaded, who only has the wardrobe to inform him that trust was never part of the job.

The films are beautiful. But some mornings, in the real world, I'm afraid something was set in motion by these people a long time ago. I can see by the way they hold hands out at the harbor. There is something unsettling about the door left open, a brief shot of a match floating in a cup of coffee,

The boat lights tacked to the sea at night with butterfly pins.

One Last Waltz on an Ave Maria

If there was music in your life, on that beach, if the wind worked the sand into loops before it pulled out the first stitch into the dark. We ran cords and portable heaters from the house to warm our legs. There's a picture I remember somewhere East, a hook of trees around a pond.

When I came home I expected to see snow, for things to be covered, for my age the passing of years to be glorified by a gifted underneath that when the thaw comes would shine again. The dilapidated garage, the alley baked in snow.

Baby trains cry in the distance.

Goldenrod bent to forward slashes. Sparrows thrown like handfuls of mud from one power line to the next. What little I had. Each gravel driveway frozen in its flow to the street.

Been praying over a jar of Miracle Whip?

I'll give you another option in a black cloak with a sickle, with a penchant for chess who fogs under cars whose shoulders are road snow; someone is painting you in their memory with no objective craft at all.

The plane high above, its cold comet's tail. It could be the first plane. Leaves blown into large curled hands. Imagine a movie from the seventies the Technicolor, the men wear corduroy and beards are athletic in a lanky way, fall in love with girls who wear no bras whose nipples point through white blouses and whose hair falls straight. Faces mangled and attractive.

There are so many things I remember about this life. A ceiling of winter clouds above the outdoor theatre. A case of bottled beer between us. Poorly tended to fire. Draw an outline around your reflection in the mirror so someone knows you died there.

In your oven is a smaller, warmer eternity. God in his pillar.
The ubiquitous woman on a lawn chair. History lesson
number one. Each daybreak comes.

You'll have children and they'll seem too heavy even at birth
to carry the weight of birth. You'll fill the bath on a cold
night and sweat, sad to know there was a time in your life
when something was decided.

Leaning closer and closer.

As if you were moving into the past, leaves un-pile across the
yard, back-flip through the air lucky and mad and hook their
leeches mouths on the trees, grow smaller. What appears to
move backwards is your failure to feel your life grow solid,
your inability to simply reel.

Frost weighing down the blades of grass. A giant American
flag over an outlet mall.

Reflected on my glasses, images of things starving and cold,
high tension wires hiss and divide the chalk blue winter sky
into highways. The little dog looks out at the wires, trying
to pinpoint the sound. I should have pitied him, but only
something more refined remembers.

We stood in the center of my room, each light from the
small mirror ball was a ring of desire's despotism. The room
is spinning again.

Beware: the dubious patriotism of the baseball bat
and the Devil and the rhubarb pie.

The way months halo around a baby's brain and darken the
edges until twenty years later she can watch a crow glide by
the fifth-story window and almost come to grips with the
legend of the failure of the great light producing machine.

A few old trailers sunk into the sides of hills.

It's not easy to believe the world is real. A significant
relationship problem: can't commit metaphysically. Not
afraid to cry, maybe cries too much. Preheated to 98.7
degrees. Can see the solution to a maze in a dog.

Strange the silence without the roar of cars and trains and
planes, mating and fighting cats
corrugated roofs and midpoints of tumbleweeds, steam from
sewer grates, steel that smiles, sun through the windows in
the state courthouse rotunda. Eventually I'll strip down to
my bones.

Won't I look funny then, won't I be difficult to rob, to stab?
Sometimes when I'm sleeping I start falling through the bed
through the night my clothes outstretched like flags, hair
raised like static.

Imagine a beach, someplace in your memory hazy enough for
meaning, blurred enough to be emotion itself stretching into
the curve of the horizon, all that dark inside, lifted somehow
into the laugh lines of waves, the one or two logs bloating
at the high tide mark, the sheen of the new night sky, that
when you look back at your life, it will seem almost nothing
was there.

Leaning closer and closer.

We were sixteen and pulled off on Southport Road because
our song came on. It comes on and on again, the memory
loss, the days grayed and lost, the pit of tar in a glace the
careful art of revolution in a smile, one second that murders
the one before with a candlestick in a room that's off the
board.

Every time I think of that scene more appears, one more
shadow of a raindrop on the dash, a heaviness in the air, a
square of skin on my arm at cold attention deep as a mistake.
Did I love you when I knew we would become other people?
Noise shot through the hands of maple leaves. Over the
dead cornfields.

One day, and this hurts to talk about, while walking through
the long practice field to high school I looked up at the gray
winter Indiana sky

and I opened. And for the first time I knew I'd never be
myself again.
The something now a *someone* in me.

We pulled off the road to kiss when our song came on. The
sun pulled under the corn-field and the night and rain came
down thick. A helix of noise swung around the TV tower. I
almost stopped! I could see noise! Noise powered from the
stereo clock's blue bones. Hurtling my silver fillings, light
from the utility trail, lives in the shadows on the dash.

The windshield began to fog. I put my mouth to yours to
move it into the shape of what I needed to say: there would
be no end to our losing, our falling, to the beach, to the gulls
in the darkening sky, to waking every morning into the same
suit of skin.

That night in the car I lost the world.

****

Many years have passed since that night. And I've learned
a rhythm to my days. That waking up involves flipping the
numerator over the denominator. That if I catch the sun at
the right angle it looks like I've been painted by an artist
who can't sleep because the sound of pipes at night makes
him feel as if he's in the belly of a half-imaged animal. And
he is.

God help me and forgive me. I was there and I wasn't there.
Forgive me, I was there and I wasn't wholly there. Forgive
me for being there. Lights of planes move across the sky,
each somnolent light drug slow.

Forgive the movement and the co-pilot and the flying.
Forgive who turned up the volume of the snow. Forgive the
soldiers, who were told to fire when they saw the whites of
eyes because there was still some idea of heaven in war, of
salvation. A storm

of white seeds came down over the polished hoods of new
Mercedes. I remember a rock club with a big metal dragon
that shot fire over the heads of the crowd, lighting their
faces in an under-worldly gold, row upon row beautiful
and frightened, each lit from within by their own separate
purgatories, their separation and the closure of themselves –
save me also,

that when I pray, I whisper, so no one but you can hear me,
for at times when I lace my hands together to open the line
it seems the biggest betrayal to ask

for another world,

another life.

Faking It

My girlfriend has multiple orgasms. I'm not sure who is
giving her these orgasms, but she'll come home with
a grocery sack and drop them on the table –

they look like tiny doorknobs made of bronze.
Neither of us is sure how they move;
they start floating in random directions
through the air, the ceiling, clouds. Stepping out

of the shower, she's beautiful. Though
if she weren't an art
so much my creation, I don't think
I'd love her at all.

At the industrial coffee shop:
of three packets of sugar – one leans against
a white mug, another the silver napkin
dispenser, and one faints on the table
like a simplistic murder scene.

My mind goes places not quite thought
on cool spring mornings when all my little infidelities
float off above the trees.

Of course, from back here nothing looks as big as it should.
not the memory I have of the large mouth bass
on the chopping block turning itself
over like an obedient coin, not the girl behind the counter
who looks so genuinely bored.

A huge parallelogram of sunlight has broken through the
window
and I feel like lying in it, silently.

Quitclaim of the Wizard of OZ

dge of reaped cornfield. Stood there. Dorothy jump-cut-materialized and ran into my arms. "What happened to the scarecrow?" she asked. "You were the scarecrow," I replied. "I knew all along," she said, brushing back her hair.

Dear Anonymous, there are small blue tornadoes in my eyes when I read your poems about the outlines of socks on your floor. Your poems entitled "Depression in a Suitcase."

On 57th street, Dorothy shook the finches out of her red scarf. I watched them spiral like a braid of colored leaves. In the background ran the EL. She had a cheese sandwich. The weather was cold. The edges of her face looked like a polygraph recording.

Coffee in Greece, heavy grounds at the bottom, the light from the poem I wrote about watermelons, the artificial womb of the bathtub, Dorothy's bare feet out of cuffed jeans, she sat on the edge of the bed, crossed her legs, and spread out her toes.

Would you trade your lion for courage?

Dear Anonymous, if I were a soldier I'd be a bad soldier because I wouldn't die for anyone or myself. May I digress? Black T-Bird blacking out. Yellow maple tree unzipped. Mattress, independent on hardwood floor.

What State is shaped like a recovering heart? What spotlight's directed screaming? What tinge of happiness as the gale numbs Dorothy's nose in the Shoe Carnival parking lot?

I put my hands in my hungry pockets. I wink back at the winking moon. Luciferian covered fingertips lighting the peach hills of Dorothy's eyelids. Rock concert in some apartment clubhouse. Girls Dorothy doesn't know on couches Dorothy doesn't know.

First you'll miss banana shakes in the summertime then
you'll learn we are voices trapped under language. Inside of
a cricket is a smaller cricket so it can hear its own Intaglio
printing, its engraving plates of purple sorrow.

Would you erase the world for a brain?
Would you trade the bashful stars above a field for a heart?

Dorothy has a golden barbecue and when she grills at night
the light waves like the bottom of a swimming pool. The
contrast of meat-smells so disturbing. Fire cares little that
it's a symbol.

Could you put up with me again, my lazy soldiering, my
annoying bullet similes: like the tears of cars, a lost tooth of
a metal shark, Death's spit?

Dorothy and I like to be alone in huge spaces, empty big box
stores, at the edge of harvested cornfields. I like to feel like
the last of my kind. This is the talking I find significant,
talking more like clothing. The broken, frozen reeds of
cornstalks, the pale, yellow sun struggling to lower its
temperature below the silos.

Would you give it all up to go home?

Nothing, Nothing

One night a man woke, not dreaming,
but standing in his socks on the heat
vent, watching the lake-effect snow dive
in long backslashes, tie and release

knots, when the present tense sharpened,
precise, isolated as a person in an empty dance hall
under the mirror ball. Soon after, he must have
drifted back to another life because

when he woke, bar candles chalked blue halos
over tables and it was summer: warm
night air loitered outside the door.
The man has a dream where he's lost

in a city, fountains on every corner,
and his map is on fire only in the places he needs to see;
it's a dream, but calmly paying
bills on quiet nights his room fills with the smoke

of years burnt away – and though he's
awake, he feels alone. By the Golden Gate,
he woke, heart a garbled mess. Birds:
motes in the sky, the air blushed with emotion

like the bursary of light inside of cathedrals
that comes from nowhere. He woke, shadows of ivy
broadcast over the bed and watched his wife's

face travel away on spectral trains. I know
how he feels, when the night hangs outside my window
like an ancient portrait and hear I the larger train
burn through the coldest places.

A Time to Sing of Airports

Before I taxi and lift away –
I'd like to touch you, drag a ring finger
up your forearm, kiss the back of your ear.
We enter moonlight like a loose door –

I mean, tonight I saw a piece of old, flat gum
dark gray on the sidewalk –
a terribly insignificant moment –

my whole life. The moon so bright, clear,
and just in that point of the desert sky
it could have been the sequestered heart
of an invisible giant. Before I carry

farther to that place, I'd like to touch you,
drag my tongue up the washboard
on the roof of your mouth. I comfort
myself on the plane by finding

the meanest looking old man and thinking,
If God takes me, he takes him also. And those
people don't die in plane wrecks;
they just evaporate from hospital beds,

the IV still swaying. There's a time to sing
about umbrellas and a time to scream
in the rain and pound on the diner window
and beg someone to hear you.

Mid-flight I worry
that if I imagined something never thought of,
say, a tiny Arabian horse in a light bulb,
that I'd accidentally trigger some ancient hex

that would shut off all machinery, plane engines,
a divine punishment for originality, a
humbling force. But the plane goes on with or
without my imagination and the tear

slides down the nectarine, and I look at
the rooftops and know it's not
about rooftops or empty theatre seats
or wearing the same pair of jeans so long
they can walk into a bar themselves

and start a fight. The *no smoking* icon dings.
Here is the lighted tennis court, here
the mouse in its panicked constitution,
here, my own blessed socks passed out on the floor

drunk with smell. Know, before I leave
I'd like to touch you, because miles below us
they are turning off the lights in the city
and it has been so long
since you've been touched.

FRANK MONTESONTI lives in San Diego and teaches creative writing in the MFA program at National University. His poems have appeared in magazines such as *Black Warrior Review*, *Poet Lore*, *Spork*, *Alaka Quarterly Review*, and *Poems and Plays*, among others.